————THE CREATIVE ART OF————

Table
Decorations

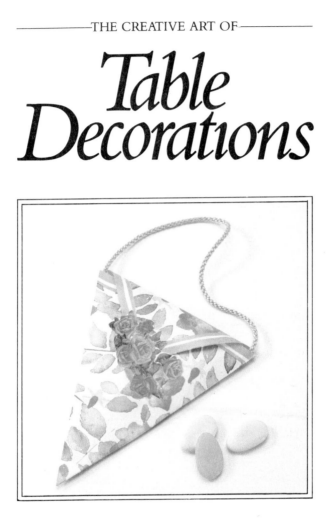

THE CREATIVE ART OF

Table Decorations

Susy Smith and Karen Lansdown

a Salamander book

Published by Salamander Books Limited
LONDON • NEW YORK

Published by Salamander Books Ltd.,
129-137 York Way, London N7 9LG,
United Kingdom.

© Salamander Books Ltd. 1987

ISBN 0 86101 291 7

Distributed in Canada by Cavendish Books Inc.,
Unit 5, 801 West 1st Street,
North Vancouver, B.C. V7P 1A4.
Phone (604) 985-2969.

All correspondence concerning the content of this volume
should be addressed to Salamander Books Ltd.

CREDITS

Editor-in-chief: Jilly Glassborow

Editor: Eleanor Van Zandt

Designer: Kathy Gummer

Photographer: Steve Tanner

Line artwork: New Leaf Designs

Typeset by: The Old Mill, London

Colour separation by: Fotographics Ltd, London – Hong Kong

Printed in Belgium by: Proost International Book Production

CONTENTS

INTRODUCTION

Entertaining at home can be fun, rewarding and, with a little extra care, a feast for the eye as well as the palate. Your guests will be delighted to find that in addition to serving them a memorable meal, you have created an individual look for the table. Simple details such as a decorative centrepiece, an unusual napkin fold or a little gift by each plate can all add to the sense of occasion.

Throughout *The Creative Book of Table Decoration* you will find suggestions for all kinds of ways to add a touch of originality to your entertaining — whether it be a formal dinner party, a buffet lunch or simply a family get-together. For easy reference the book is divided into sections, each dealing with a different aspect of table decoration: centrepieces, napkins, tablecloths and placemats, place cards, and gifts. Each section contains a wealth of ideas, and in every case a detailed step-by-step guide shows how easy the various items are to make.

Apart from the creative aspect of table settings there are, of course, many practicalities to be considered: what to look for when buying china, cutlery and glassware, and how best to care for them; when to use a decanter and which wines to serve with different foods; when to apply the formal rules of etiquette; and how to arrange cutlery and glasses. All of these questions and more are answered and will help to make entertaining a pleasure for you and your guests.

——TABLE DECORATION——

When you invite guests to dinner, good food is obviously the first and foremost consideration; however, its presentation is also important. This should apply to everything from the atmosphere created by the lighting to the china on which the food is served and the way the table is set. You don't necessarily have to own starched damask cloths, cut glass and bone china to lay a decorative table; the most important requirements are enthusiasm and a little ingenuity. Indeed, table settings created on a budget often look more inventive and unusual than those with a conventional approach. Throughout this book many of the ideas use materials that are inexpensive and easy to buy — and, in many cases, things that you may already have around the house.

——TABLE DESIGN——

Choosing the right tableware can be difficult. Do you look for a style that is contemporary and unusual and that matches your current colour scheme, or do you choose classic designs which won't date and will go with anything? There are advantages to both approaches. Your choice will ultimately depend largely on how much you've got to spend and how strong a statement you wish to make.

It is important to find a starting point on which to base the style and colour of your tableware. Inspiration will usually come from the existing colour scheme and furnishings in the room where you eat. China, table linen, and, these days, even cutlery can be chosen to match, or contrast with, walls, carpet or fabrics.

If your dining table is made of beautiful wood — either solid or veneer — you may choose individual placemats, rather than covering it up with cloth. In a traditional dining room placemats often feature reproductions of old prints, such as hunting scenes. On an antique pine table, cork or raffia mats enhance the rustic image. Placemats for a modern table should be as plain and unobtrusive as possible to remain in keeping with the streamlined look.

If you prefer a tablecloth to mats, but can't find one to co-ordinate with your decor or china, you can buy a length of fabric and make your own tablecloth by hemming the edges. Depending on the size of your table, it may be necessary to join two widths of fabric; in this case, a 'busy' print is preferable to a solid colour, on which a seam is more noticeable.

When selecting china, remember that apart from looking good on the table it must also show food to its best advantage. If you are in

A sumptuous design such as this does not have to be expensive; it owes more to a can of gold spray paint and a little ingenuity than to large amounts of money.

doubt, it may be worthwhile buying one plate from the service you like and trying it out at home with food on it to see whether or not it is suitable. One idea, which is popular in the United States and with some British restauranteurs, is to use an underplate. This is larger than a dinner plate and can remain at a place setting throughout the meal, with the plate or bowl for each course being set on top of it. Because underplates never have food actually served on them, they can be highly patterned or a strong, plain colour, and thus prove the perfect foil for a plain white or more subtly coloured dinner service. And when you want to create a different look, you can just replace your underplates with another colour or pattern. In the gold table setting (above) a large white underplate sprayed with gold aerosol paint adds a touch of opulence to white linen and china.

Cutlery these days comes in many different shapes, sizes and colours and should be chosen to complement your china. Coloured handles can look attractive but may become a limitation if you decide to change your colour scheme. Again, the best solution may be to go for something fairly simple and use decorative accessories, such as flowers and coloured napkins, to brighten up the table.

Having acquired the essentials, you can turn your attention to the decorative touches — of which you will find many examples in the pages of this book.

BUYING AND CARING
FOR TABLEWARE

The choice of tableware available today is vast, and there are ranges to suit all tastes and budgets. For practical reasons it is often best to buy inexpensive items for everyday use. You can spend more on a range of tableware that is to be kept for special occasions and entertaining. If the design you like seems rather expensive, remember that most china, cutlery and glassware can be bought as individual pieces or in place settings, so you don't have to buy it all at once. Your collection can be built up over a period of time; in this case, however, it is important to choose designs that are not about to be discontinued.

GLASSWARE

There are literally hundreds of glassware designs to choose from today, from intricately cut lead crystal to the simplest glass tumbler. Prices vary enormously and are generally higher for hand-made than for machine-made glass. The most expensive hand-made glass is 'full' lead crystal, which contains about 30% lead oxide. Lead crystal contains slightly less oxide and is thus cheaper; lead glass is the third grade. Because of its high degree of light refraction, lead crystal is ideal for decorative cutting, which displays this refracting property to the best advantage. Increasingly popular these days is re-cycled glass, with its distinctive greenish hue and suspended bubbles. It is thicker than other types of glass and has a charming rustic quality.

Rules about which glasses to use are much less rigid today than in the past, and it is not necessary to have a large range. You can get by with only three kinds of glass: tumblers, which can be used for spirits, beer or water; medium- or large-sized wineglasses (those that curve inward slightly at the top are preferred by wine experts); and a set of small glasses, stemmed or tumbler-shaped, which will do for sherry, port and even liqueurs. Balloon brandy glasses are a useful extra; they, too, can be used for liqueurs. If you're investing in champagne glasses, buy the narrow flute type, rather the the wide ones, which dissipate the bouquet. If you wish to buy a fuller range of glasses, the table opposite will help you to identify the various types.

Great care should be taken when washing glasses, for they can easily chip. Lead crystal, and indeed most hand-made glasses, should always be washed by hand. Also, glasses washed in a dishwasher will eventually become milky in appearance; however, if your glasses were not too expensive, you may be prepared to sacrifice their longevity for the sake of convenience.

Sherry White wine Red wine Champagne

Port Whisky Highball

Brandy Cocktail Liqueur

CHINA AND POTTERY

China is a term generally applied to a variety of different materials. However, there are two main groups: true china, or porcelain, and pottery. Porcelain is made of kaolin, or china clay, which is sometimes almost translucent. Bone china is a combination of china clay, stone and bone ash, which makes it extremely tough, despite its delicate appearance. Fine china is expensive, although if treated with care it will last a lifetime. It must be heated gently; if it is placed in a hot oven the glaze will become crazed and the fine sheen will disappear. Hand-painted china or designs decorated with gold or silver should always be washed by hand, for dishwashers will, in time, damage the decoration. Similarly, fine china should never be placed in a microwave oven; not only can this damage the decoration; it is also detrimental to the microwave.

The two main kinds of pottery, stoneware and earthenware, are heavier and thicker than porcelain, or china, and vary in quality, design and price. Unglazed earthenware is porous, will often chip easily and cannot withstand extreme oven heat. Glazed earthenware is more durable, but stoneware is by far the toughest type of pottery and can be used in the oven as well as on the table. Today there are also many ranges of specially toughened oven-to-table ware, some of which can also be used in the freezer.

If you own a dishwasher, this will be a prime consideration when choosing china. The manufacturer will usually state whether or not a particular line is dishwasher-proof. As a general guide, anything that is hand-made, hand-painted or unglazed must be washed by hand.

It is advisable to use either a plastic washing-up bowl or a rubber mat in the sink to prevent chips and breakages. Instead of scraping plates with a knife to remove food, wipe them with paper towels, or with your hands (you should always wear rubber gloves to protect your hands when washing dishes). A soft cloth or sponge is best for washing china and glasses, although you may need a soft brush for removing crumbs from crevices. Always soak cooking utensils and tableware immediately after use to remove any particles of food before they become hard to dislodge.

CUTLERY

For cutlery the choice is between stainless steel, silverplate and sterling silver. Some cutlery has traditional bone or wooden handles; and many modern ranges feature coloured acrylic handles. These can look attractive when co-ordinated with china and table linen but restrict

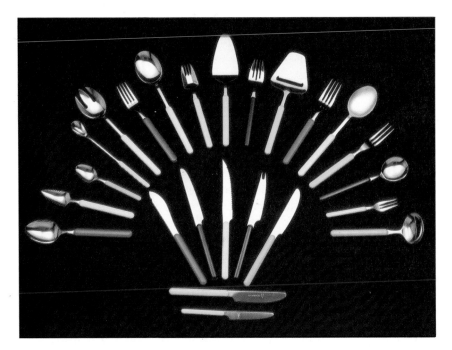

This colourful display of modern cutlery shows some of the possibilities available if you wish to colour-co-ordinate your china and cutlery. However, traditional silver or stainless steel is more versatile.

your choice if you decide to change your colour scheme. Cutlery with carved or moulded handles should not be washed in a dishwasher, for the handles can become loose or damaged. Even when washing by hand it is wise not to immerse the handles of the cutlery in water for long periods. All cutlery should be dried as soon as possible after washing to prevent water spots.

TABLE LINEN

Traditional tablecloths in white linen or cotton damask are still available, but they are expensive and must be properly laundered to maintain their colour and finish. More practical, particularly for everyday use, is polyester or a polyester-cotton blend. Easy to wash and iron, polyester is the ideal material for the modern household where time is at a premium. PVC, or vinyl, is another practical material for cloths, especially in families with small children. Tablemats are a trouble-free alternative, since most have wipe-clean surfaces.

TABLE SETTINGS

A more relaxed approach to table settings these days means that you are unlikely to encounter a table laid for a five-course meal unless attending some kind of formal function. However, to avoid feeling intimidated by a place setting flanked with rows of cutlery and glasses, it is useful to know what to expect on such an occasion.

FORMAL SETTINGS

The basic rule for cutlery, working from the outside in, will usually apply. For a meal with five courses in Britain, one would expect to see a small bread or hors d'oeuvre knife on the outside right, then a soup spoon; next to this a fish knife, then a large table knife for meat or poultry, and last of all a dessert spoon. On the left would be a small fork for hors d'oeuvre, then a fish fork, a larger fork for meat or poultry and finally a dessert fork. To avoid having too many pieces of cutlery on the table at the start of the meal, some courses may have cutlery brought to the table when they are served. This applies particularly to special dishes such as snails, crab and lobster.

A similar system is used in the United States, except that instead of having a dessert spoon and fork next to the plate, there is a small fork and knife used for salad and cheese respectively, such courses preceding the dessert. The dessert spoons and forks are brought to the table along

A formal place setting for a five-course dinner in Britain has all the cutlery arranged at either side of the plate. There are usually four glasses: one each for sherry, white wine, red wine and champagne.

with the dessert and, sometimes, finger bowls.

Four glasses will normally be arranged at the top right-hand corner of each place setting. These are used in the opposite order to the cutlery. Working from the inside out, you will find, first, a sherry glass (sherry is served with the soup); next comes a small wineglass for white wine, then a large wine glass for red wine and, finally, a champagne flute (champagne accompanies the dessert). A large goblet for water may be placed behind these four glasses.

INFORMAL SETTINGS

These formal rules are not often adhered to when entertaining at home, partly because most dining tables are not large enough to accommodate this amount of glassware and cutlery. It is much more important that your guests feel at ease than that they follow any strict formal procedure. A compromise for a meal with several courses is to place the butter knife across the side plate, to the left of the setting. A soup spoon or implements for hors d'oeuvres can be placed in readiness on the relevant dish as it is served. In Britain the dessert fork and spoon are generally placed nose to tail across the top of the setting. Thus only four pieces of cutlery are placed beside the setting — a fish knife and fork, and inside these a table knife and fork for the meat

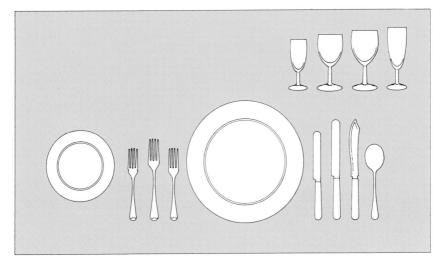

The formal place setting differs slightly in the United States, in that the dessert spoon and fork are brought in with the dessert plate and fingerbowl. The inner fork and knife are for the salad and cheese courses, served before the dessert.

dish. The choice of cutlery will, of course, vary according to the menu. And in the United States the dessert cutlery will be brought in with the dessert, rather than being placed above the plate.

SERVING AND SEATING

Seating arrangements are important, if only so that guests can take their places at the table with a minimum of fuss. Place cards are an ideal solution here and can be an attractive embellishment to each place setting. Otherwise it is up to the host and hostess to direct the guests to their seats. Formal etiquette requires the host and hostess to sit facing one another — at the far ends of the table, if it is rectangular. The female guest of honour sits to the right of the host, the male guest of honour sits to the right of the hostess. For informal entertaining, however, the seating arrangements are usually based on providing a good mix of people around the table to stimulate conversation. Alternating male and female guests is usual, and partners are not seated next to one another. It may be impossible or irrelevant to apply these rules, especially if the numbers of each sex are different. You may prefer to seat your guests next to others they will get on with or with whom they have something in common. As a rule it is best for the host and hostess to be in the seats with the most

For less formal occasions the butter knife can be placed on the side plate, and the first course cutlery can be placed on the dish as the food is served. In Britain the dessert cutlery is placed above the plate.

convenient access to the kitchen, in order to avoid disturbing guests when serving food and drinks.

Food should be served to the left of guests, plates removed from the right. The female guest of honour is served first, and the other guests are served in order of age or importance. A more informal and convenient plan may be to serve clockwise around the table. The host and hostess should always be served last. At formal dinners in Britain no-one is permitted to smoke before the toast to the Queen. On any occasion, smoking between courses should be discouraged, for the benefit of non-smokers and also because this may delay the serving of subsequent courses and mean continual emptying of ashtrays.

Traditionally in Britain port is served with cheese at the end of the meal. The bottle or decanter is passed around the table from left to right, and people should be left to help themselves. Formal etiquette states that the bottle should not be set down on the table until it has completed the round. Brandy and liqueurs are served with coffee, and on formal occasions cigars are also offered at this point. This is the time when guests should be permitted to smoke. Coffee can be served at the table; or guests can retire to the living room for it. This can sometimes interrupt the flow of conversation; on the other hand it can allow guests to mingle more freely. It is really up to the host and hostess to decide which of these alternatives will better suit the occasion.

The diagram on the right shows the seating arrangement for a formal dinner. The host and hostess sit at opposite ends of the table, the host with the female guest of honour to his right and the hostess with the male guest of honour to her right. Couples do not sit together but are placed diagonally opposite each other. The arrangement is as follows: A) Host; B) Female; C) Male; D) Female; E) Male guest of honour; F) Hostess; G) Male; H) Female; I) Male; J) Female guest of honour.

FOOD AND WINE

The formal rules about which wines should be served with which foods have become much more relaxed these days, and often the same wine is served throughout the meal. For more formal occasions, however, the following guidelines may be useful. With most first courses, cold dishes, fish or white meat in a white sauce, you should serve a white wine (either dry or medium), or perhaps a rosé. A light red wine can be served with white meat dishes when they are in a dark sauce. A fuller-bodied red wine is served with more strongly flavoured red meat dishes, such as stews, casseroles, grills and roasts. There are also sweet wines, such as sauterne, which can be served with the dessert at the end of a meal, although many people prefer a demi-sec champagne. Basically the wine should be complementary to the dish; the richer the food, the fuller the wine should be. It is important not to allow a light, delicate dish to be overpowered by a heavy wine, nor a delicate wine to be overpowered by too rich a dish.

Red wine should be served at room temperature, and white wines should be served chilled. The definition of room temperature is approximately 16°C (61°F). If the wine has been in a cellar, it should be brought up to the correct temperature gradually, not heated quickly — say, by standing it on a stove. White wine should be chilled to a temperature of about 6-8°C (43-46°F); too cold a temperature will subdue the full flavour. Red wines should be uncorked and allowed to stand for about an hour before serving. If you are serving a fine old red

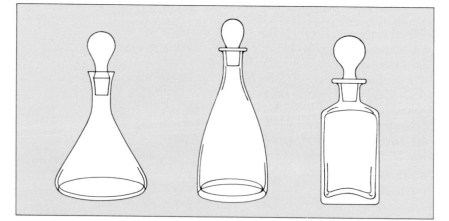

Traditional styles of decanter: on the left, a ship's decanter, originally designed for stability at sea but popular on land as well, for wine, port or sherry; centre, another classic shape for wines; right, a square decanter for whisky and other spirits.

wine, it will usually need to be decanted; this separates the wine from its sediment and allows it to 'breathe'. When decanting wine, allow the bottle to stand upright for a few hours to let the sediment settle. Then, in one movement, pour the wine into a clean, dry decanter without allowing any of the sediment to leave the bottle. Holding the bottle in front of a light source allows you to see when the sediment is reaching the neck.

APERITIFS AND LIQUEURS

It is customary to offer your guests a drink before their meal. Traditionally, this is either sherry, vermouth, whisky, or a cocktail, but often today guests will ask for wine. Essentially an apéritif should have a fresh, clean taste in order to whet a person's appetite for the meal to come.

After the meal, often with coffee, it is usual to offer a liqueur, port or brandy. To enhance the flavour of a fine brandy, such as cognac, warm the glasses slightly before pouring the brandy. Balloon brandy glasses can also be used for liqueurs and are easier to handle than tiny liqueur glasses; but take care not to over-pour, since these sweet liquids can be cloying. Today some people prefer liqueurs with ice, which serves as a foil to the richness of the drink.

Every table needs a focal point, and this is, more often than not, in the centre. The usual choice for a centrepiece is a flower arrangement or a bowl of fruit, but occasionally it is fun to dream up something a little more unusual or exotic. The important thing to remember is that although a centrepiece should be large enough to make a statement, it should never take over the table, leaving little room for anything else and forcing your guests to peer around it to talk to one another! In this section you will discover how to make a wide range of centrepieces, some purely decorative and some edible.

Although designed for a wedding
reception, this table setting would also be
suitable for a special dinner party. The
look is pretty and lacy, and the
centrepiece picks up the apricot and white
colour scheme. The apricots can be eaten
at the end of the meal, provided they are
kept separate from the poisonous ivy
leaves by a paper doily.

APRICOTS AND CREAM

A mound of luscious apricots, flowers and leaves makes a pretty centrepiece for a summer buffet or dinner party. Place a white doily on a glass or china cake stand. Carefully push ivy leaves underneath the edge of the doily. The leaves should be washed and can be wiped with cooking oil for extra shine.

Holding the doily in place with one hand, arrange the apricots in a pile. (If the apricots are to be eaten, do not allow them to touch the ivy leaves, which are poisonous.) Then arrange a few sprays of cream-coloured freesias around the pile of apricots.

Finally, slot flowers into the gaps between the apricots — any small cream or white flowers will do; those used here are narcissi. Check with your florist that the flowers you choose are not poisonous.

For an unusual Easter centre-piece fill a rustic basket with a selection of different eggs. The basket shown contains a mixture of hen's eggs, tiny speckled quail's eggs (which can be eaten as an hors d'oeuvre), and carved wooden eggs. Half fill the basket with paper to form a base for the eggs, then add a layer of packing straw.

Arrange your selection of eggs in the packing straw to show off their different colours and patterns. Tie a ribbon around the handle of the basket to provide a finishing touch.

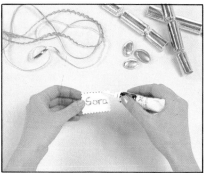

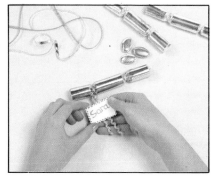

These attractive miniature crackers form an eye catching centrepiece, and the surrounding sweets make a delicious accompaniment to coffee at the end of the meal. For the name tags, cut small squares and rectangles from white cardboard. Trim the edges decoratively, then write the names and embellish the edges of the card with silver or gold paint.

Cut lengths of gold and silver ribbon or braid about 15cm (6in) long. Tie a ribbon around one end of each cracker. Dab a spot of glue on the back of each name tag and press it onto the ribbon.

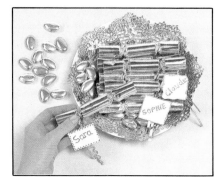

Pile the crackers onto a large plate covered with a gold doily. Place those with name cards near the top of the pile. For a finishing touch, surround the pile of crackers with gold and silver dragées.

A touch of gold gives this platter of fruit and nuts extra richness. Begin by spraying ivy, clementines, bay leaves and fir cones with gold paint. (If the fruit will be eaten, make sure that the paint you are using is non-toxic.)

Place the ivy leaves around the edge of a plain oval platter. The flatter the plate, the better, for this will allow the ivy leaves to hang over the edge.

Arrange the clementines on the platter, surround them with dates and nuts, and place a bunch of shiny black grapes on top. Add the gold leaves and fir cones for a luxurious finishing touch.

This stunning centrepiece looks
grand enough to grace the most
formal dinner party, and yet is very
simple to make. Using a pastry
brush, coat each piece of fruit with
egg white.

Working over a large plate, sprinkle
granulated sugar over the fruit so
that it adheres to the coating of egg.
Alternatively, the fruit can be dipped
into a bowl of sugar, although this
tends to make the sugar lumpy.

Ivy leaves are used here to form a
decorative border; but remember to
use a doily to separate the poisonous
leaves from the fruit if you intend to
eat the fruit later.

This elegant candle-ring is the ideal centrepiece for a special dinner party at any time of the year. A circular cake base serves as the foundation for the arrangement. Begin by attaching strands of ivy to the edge of the base, securing them with drawing pins.

Build up the ring by adding more strands and bunches of leaves until only a small space remains in the centre. Push stems of freesia among the ivy leaves to provide colour contrast.

Use a mixture of white and green candles of varying heights to form the centre of the arrangement. Secure each candle to the base with a blob of glue or Plasticine (modelling clay).

This festive wreath is ideal if you're short of space on the table — it can be suspended from a hook screwed into the ceiling. Use wire cutters to snip the hook off a coat hanger. Bend the hanger into a circular shape. Bunch damp sphagnum moss around the wire to a thickness of about 5cm (2in), using gardener's wire around it to hold it in place.

Take several bushy branches of evergreen, such as cypress, and arrange them to cover the circlet of moss, overlapping the pieces to cover any stalks. Tie the branches to the ring with gardener's twine or wire.

Add several sprigs of holly, again securing them with wire. If the holly is a bit short of berries, you can add some fake berries at this point.

To hang the wreath you will need two lengths of satin ribbon. Each piece should be twice the length of the drop from the ceiling to your hanging height, plus an extra 20cm (8in) for tying around the wreath. Tie each of the four ends opposite one another around the wreath so that the two lengths cross in the centre.

Make four bows from the same colour ribbon and pin them to the wreath over the four tying-on points.

Gently push a length of florist's wire through each of four red wax candles, approximately 1.5cm (½in) above the bases, as shown.

Position each candle halfway between two bows, and twist the wire around the wreath to hold it in place. To hang the wreath, tie another length of ribbon around the two main ribbons where they cross, make a loop to go over the hook, and tie the ends in a bow.

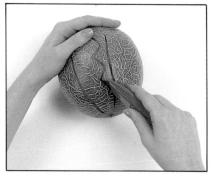

This clever centrepiece not only looks scrumptious but can be served for dessert at the end of the meal. Using a sharp knife, cut strips out of the melon skin to create a pattern all over it. Take care not to cut too deeply into the skin. Discard the cut-out pieces.

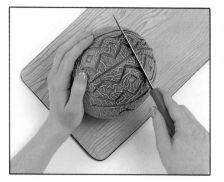

Having completed the design, place the melon on a chopping board. With a sharp kitchen knife slice the top off the melon; set it aside.

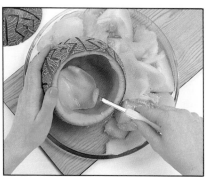

Scoop out the flesh of the melon onto a plate. Discard the seeds and slice or cube the melon flesh. Mix this with other fruits to create a salad, and return it to the melon bowl. Garnish it with mint leaves. Place the melon on a plate, and surround it with a selection of other fruits.

Fruit is often used as a centre-piece, and here an attractive effect has been created by hand-painting a plain wicker basket to match the colour of the fruit. Paint the basket inside and out with a water-based paint in the background colour, using a small decorating brush. Leave the basket to dry.

Dip a sponge into a saucer containing the contrasting colour of paint. Dab the sponge a few times on a piece of scrap paper to remove any excess. Then sponge all over the outside of the basket, replenishing your paint supply when necessary.

Arrange the fruit in the basket as shown, adding a few leaves for contrast. Clementines are shown here, but apples, bananas and other fruit could be added for variety.

This autumnal arrangement of dried flowers makes an appropriate centrepiece for a Thanksgiving or Harvest Festival dinner. Begin by placing a square of florists' foam in the basket. Create a skirt-shaped outline around the basket using dried wheat ears or grasses. Begin to build up the arrangement by adding some poppy heads.

Fill in the shape with larger dried flowers, such as this gold-coloured yarrow.

Twist lengths of florists' wire around fir cones to give them 'stalks'. Insert the stalks into the oasis.

Using a selection of different-shaped dried flowers, such as this statice, fill in the remaining gaps to balance the arrangement.

Add a few white daisies to provide highlights. (White flowers can often be used to lighten the effect of a flower arrangement — dried or fresh.)

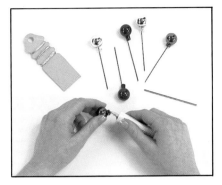

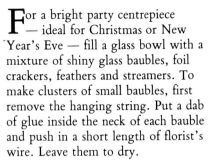

For a bright party centrepiece — ideal for Christmas or New Year's Eve — fill a glass bowl with a mixture of shiny glass baubles, foil crackers, feathers and streamers. To make clusters of small baubles, first remove the hanging string. Put a dab of glue inside the neck of each bauble and push in a short length of florist's wire. Leave them to dry.

Hold the wired baubles in a cluster and wind fine fuse wire around the stems to hold them together.

Wrap a piece of shiny giftwrap ribbon around the stems and tie it into a bow. Arrange the baubles and other ornaments in the bowl as shown.

This pretty centrepiece is a good wintertime alternative to a vase of real flowers. Lay a sheet of coloured tissue between two different-coloured layers of net. Place a vase in the centre of the net and tissue, and gather the three layers up around the neck of the vase.

Secure the net and tissue in place with a piece of twine or an elastic band. Tie a length of contrasting wide satin ribbon in a bow around the neck of the vase.

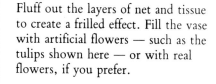

Fluff out the layers of net and tissue to create a frilled effect. Fill the vase with artificial flowers — such as the tulips shown here — or with real flowers, if you prefer.

This simple centrepiece can be made up using any colours of candles and marbles; choose the colours to co-ordinate with your table linen and china. To fix the candles in place, light one and drip some hot wax onto the plate. Before the wax dries, stand a candle on top of it; this will hold the candle securely.

When all the candles have been arranged in a group, surround them with a 'sea' of marbles. Take care to put the marbles in place gently, for they may crack the plate if dropped onto it.

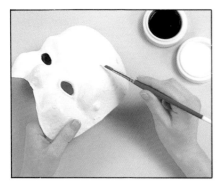

These unusual harlequin masks form the perfect party centre-piece, especially when co-ordinated with a black and white table setting, as shown on pages 96-97. The masks can be bought or home-made from *papier mâché*. Paint each mask white.

With a pencil draw diagonal lines across the mask to create a grid. Don't worry if the squares are not exactly symmetrical. Paint alternate squares black.

Glue a length of black lace or net around the edge of the mask. Add coloured feathers and ribbons for the finishing touches. Stand the masks back to back so that one is facing each side of the table.

MARZIPAN FRUIT PARCELS

Exquisite marzipan fruits deserve special presentation. Nestling in little tissue 'parcels' and piled into a cake stand, they make a colourful centrepiece. All you need is several different colours of tissue paper and some pinking shears. Instead of marzipan fruits, you could use chocolates or marrons glacés.

From a double layer of one colour of tissue, cut a 10cm (4in) square. Pinking shears give an attractive serrated edge. From another colour of tissue, also double, cut a smaller square, measuring about 6cm (2½in).

Lay the smaller square on top of the larger one. Place the marzipan fruit in the centre and gather the tissue around it. Hold it in place for a few seconds and then let go; the crumpled tissue will retain its rosette shape. Place several of the parcels on a doily-lined glass or china cake stand.

These individual cakes, each with its own candle, make an unusual alternative to a large birthday cake for a children's party and form an attractive centrepiece. Decorate each cake with a pattern, or pipe a child's name onto it.

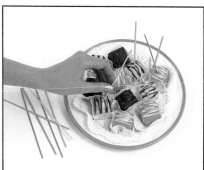

Stick a long taper candle into each cake and arrange the cakes on a large plate. Once lit, the candles should not be allowed to burn for too long, as the hot wax will begin to drop onto the cakes.

Candles can always be relied on to lend atmosphere to any occasion. For a co-ordinated effect, paint plain terracotta or glazed candlesticks to match your colour scheme. You will need water-based paint for terracotta candlesticks and ceramic paint for glazed ones. Give the candlestick two coats of base colour, using a soft, narrow artist's paintbrush.

Use one or more contrasting colours to decorate the holder. If using a lighter colour on a dark base, paint the design in white first and colour in afterwards. Sponging or spattering the base coat with a contrasting colour would look equally attractive.

For a summer table centrepiece nothing can surpass the beauty of flowers. The secret of successful flower arranging is a careful choice of containers and a harmonious colour scheme. When using several containers, try to get a variety of shapes. The jugs used here have contrasting forms but similar colours; the flowers include shades of pink, white and red.

The tall jug contains a mixture of anemones, ranunculus, kaffir lily (*Schizostylis*) and white September flowers, the mixture of shapes providing variety. The smallest vase contains a tiny narcissi, ranunculus and anemones with a few sprigs of love-in-a-mist (*Nigella*). The deep red anemone at the front serves as a focal point.

This fat, rounded jug has a fairly wide neck and is therefore ideal for full-blown roses, which look good clustered together to form a close, rounded shape. Delicate stalks of white September flowers (aster) and a few heads of love-in-a-mist show up well against the pale pink roses and give more definition to the arrangement.

A delightful idea for a spring or Easter centrepiece, these pretty floral baskets are easy to make and will last much longer than cut flowers. First line the basket with a piece of plastic, using black for a dark twig basket or white for a light-coloured willow basket.

Add a layer of damp sphagnum moss. This will provide a base for your pots of flowers, lifting them to the correct height for the basket. It also prevents the roots of the plants from drying out. (Check the moss occasionally to make sure it is still damp; if not, sprinkle it with water to dampen it.)

Arrange the pots on top of the layer of moss, adjusting them if necessary so that they relate well to each other.

You can leave the basket plain or, as shown here, add a paper doily for a pretty trim. Cut two doilies in half and fold the edge of each half around the rim of the basket before inserting the pots.

Tie ribbons around the handle of each basket to provide the finishing touch.

This colourful fruit salad not only makes an eyecatching centrepiece but also can be served for a refreshing dessert. Set aside the best-looking fruit to decorate the edges of the container — in this case, kiwi fruit and several large strawberries. Cut up the remaining strawberries, and peel and section the tangerines.

Then peel and slice the kiwi fruit. Layer the fruit into a square or oblong glass container, placing the slices and segments flat against the glass to form a pattern with the different shapes.

Peel and thickly slice the remaining kiwi fruit into three pieces, and then slice again down the centre, stopping halfway. Slice the strawberries down the middle, stopping 1 cm ($^3/_8$in) short of the stalk. Slide the fruit onto the edge of the glass, either in two rows as shown or alternating all the way around.

Although flowers are most often arranged in vases, it is just as easy to create a pretty centrepiece using ordinary containers you may have around the house. This natural, yet graceful, arrangement uses a mixture of spring flowers in jam jars. A few coloured glass bottles are added for contrast.

Here a squat clear jar is used for a mixture of white flowers and silvery-green foliage, forming a cool two-colour arrangement.

A single hyacinth is enough to fill the smaller jar, and the twisted stem of an anemone fits perfectly into a thin blue glass bottle. A colourful bunch of anemones in another jam jar completes the centrepiece.

This charming informal centre-piece is proof that flowers can be arranged effectively in all sorts of containers. In fact, an unusual container often adds interest to a simple flower arrangement. The two shown here are a pretty floral mug and a wide cup and saucer, the kind used for breakfast coffee in France.

Tulips are usually arranged in a tall vase, but this is often too tall for a centrepiece. Here they are treated more informally, grouped in a pretty mug. Cut the stems short to suit the container, but don't discard the leaves — arrange them in among the flowers. The breakfast cup is first partially filled with freesias.

A few carefully placed anemones add colour to the arrangement and also help to link it with the tulips in the other container.

─── *FLOATING FLOWERS* ───

Flowers are definite favourites when it comes to centrepieces, so here's an attractive variation on a theme. Use a wide-necked bowl, either glass or ceramic, and fill it with water to about 2cm (1in) below the rim. Then, snipping their stalks off close to the head, arrange some flowers on the surface of the water.

Flowers with large heads, such as the tulips and roses used here, are the easiest kind to float. But a few small orchids, with their interesting outline, add contrast to the arrangement.

Finally, add three or four floating candles. (Be careful not to overload the bowl with flowers, for they could catch fire once the candles are lit!)

This beautiful centrepiece is worthy of a wedding supper; and it's not too difficult for an amateur flower arranger. First place a block of oasis in the centre of a large salver. Make a 'skirt' around the edge by sticking laurel leaves horizontally into the base of the oasis. Add some eucalyptus sprays to build up the shape.

When you have created a triangular shape of eucalyptus and laurel, add sprays of white gladiolus and arum lilies to contrast with the greenery. In placing these, aim for a balanced effect, beginning with a lily in the centre and working out and around. Remember that the arrangement will be seen from all sides, so keep turning it to check for gaps.

Next, insert sprays of chrysanthemum and white lilac among the other white flowers. Keep checking all sides of the arrangement to maintain the balance.

The final colour contrast is provided
by tulips and roses in varying shades
of pink. Here again it is important to
maintain symmetry, so work around
the arrangement, filling in where
colour is lacking. Allow some of the
blooms to lie over the edge of the
salver by pushing their stalks
horizontally into the oasis.

These small fir trees are fun to decorate and add a festive touch to any Christmas sideboard or buffet table. For the gold tree, make small bows of fine gold ribbon. Drape a string of gold beads in a spiral over the tree, starting at the top, then fix the bows in between the loops of beads.

Wrap some tartan ribbon around the pot and secure the ends with fabric glue. Make a separate bow and attach it with glue or pins.

For the red tree, cut fine ribbon into 15cm (6in) lengths, tie them into bows and position them on the tree as shown.

Tie some tiny red ornaments to the branches; or, if the tree is dense enough, simply place them in the spaces between the bows. Add a wide red ribbon sash around the terracotta pot, tying it in a big bow.

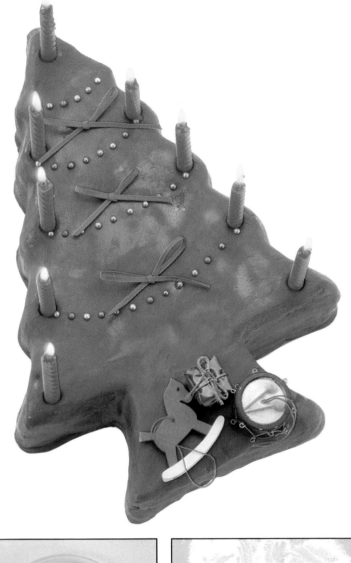

This festive Christmas tree cake will be the featured attraction at a Christmas tea. The cake can be made to your own traditional recipe and should be baked in a Christmas tree cake tin. The simplest method for icing the cake is to use ready-to-roll fondant icing. Knead the block into a ball and work in some green food colouring.

Roll the coloured icing out flat on a cool surface, first sprinkling some icing, or confectioner's, sugar on the worktop to prevent the icing from sticking.

Carefully roll the sheet of icing over the rolling pin and unroll it onto the cake. Shape the icing around the cake, keeping your hands wet to smooth out any cracks.

Add rows of edible cake balls to suggest garlands draped across the tree.

Place tiny red ribbon bows on the cake. (You can use a glass-headed pin to secure the bows, but take care to remove them all before serving the cake.)

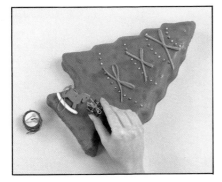

Place a selection of 'presents' around the bottom of the tree — the ones used here are Christmas tree decorations.

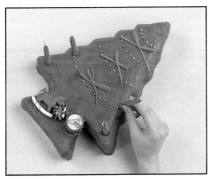

Push red wax candles into the icing around the edges of the tree to complete the effect.

Except in hotels and restaurants, table linen is not used as often these days as it used to be. For convenience, many people have turned to heat-resistant, wipe-clean placemats. This is a shame, because starched white table linen has an elegance that can never be matched. There are, however, attractive alternatives to the traditional damask cloth; many tablecloths now have easy-care finishes, which simplify the laundering. For a special occasion it is fun to use a cloth — or placemat — in keeping with a particular theme or design, such as those included in the following pages.

Although designed for a Thanksgiving or
Harvest Festival dinner, this setting could
be used at any time of the year. The
'placemat' is really an outline printed on
a plain white cloth, using a potato cut in
a leaf shape; the napkin uses the same
motif. Wooden-handled cutlery, hand-
blown glass and dried flowers help to set
the rustic theme.

Why not decorate a plain white tablecloth with a placemat outline to match your china? All you need is a raw potato and some paint. First cut the potato into a cube about the size of your chosen motif. The leaf shape shown here is about 3cm (1¼in) square. Using a sharp knife, cut the motif on one side of the cube as shown.

Use a paint suitable for fabric, or a water-based paint if you are printing on a paper tablecloth. Spread the paint evenly over the raised motif.

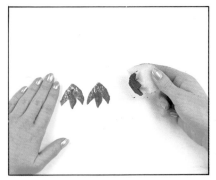

On a piece of stiff paper, draw the outline of the 'placemat' in black felt-tip pen. Place this under the cloth as a guide when printing. Press the potato down onto the cloth, taking care not to smudge it. Practice first on a spare piece of paper. The same technique can be used to print a border design around the edge of the napkin.

This pretty tablecloth isn't hard to make but requires a bit of patience. You can make the cloth yourself or buy one ready-made. Buy enough ribbon in each colour to run along four sides of the cloth, plus 24cm (8in) if using a ready-made cloth. Position the ribbons as shown, with fusible webbing underneath (omitting the area where they will cross), and pin them in place.

Continue to pin the ribbons in place along all the edges, making sure that you keep them straight. Thread the ribbons underneath one another to create a lattice effect, as shown. If you are using a ready-made cloth, allow the ribbons to overlap the edge by 3cm (1in); this will be folded under later.

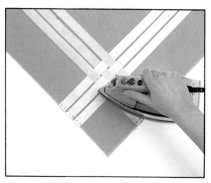

Replace the corner pins with tacking (basting) stitches, if you are working on an un-hemmed cloth; this provides extra stability. Press the ribbons in place with a warm iron, removing pins as you go and stopping just short of the tacking. Finally, hem the edges. On a ready-made cloth, sew the ribbon ends to the wrong side by hand.

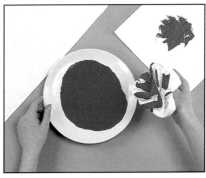

Rag-rolling, or ragging, is a quick and easy way to transform a plain fabric or paper tablecloth. Pour a water-based paint or fabric dye onto a plate, and dip a crumpled piece of cloth in it. Blot the cloth on some waste paper or fabric to remove excess paint.

Lightly press the crumpled fabric onto a spare piece of paper or cloth to practice getting an even amount of paint over the area to be covered. Once you feel confident, rag the tablecloth, adding a second colour (once the first has dried) if desired. If using fabric dye, follow the manufacturer's instructions for fixing the colour.

ABSTRACT TABLECLOTH

Transform a plain tablecloth with this eyecatching design. Choose a brush the correct size for your design, and use a paint suitable for fabrics. (Because the paint is applied quite thickly, a paper tablecloth is not suitable.)

Practice first on a spare piece of cloth or paper, dipping the brush into the paint for each new stroke. Then paint the cloth, applying the lighter colour first; allow it to dry thoroughly.

Paint on the second colour in broad sweeps, allowing the paint to fade off towards the end of each brushstroke. Follow the manufacturer's instructions for fixing the fabric paint.

A dd a touch of luxury to a
dinner party by decorating your
own tablecloth in gold. First choose
a simple image, such as the fleur-de-
lys motif shown here. You can either
decorate an existing cloth or buy a
length of wide inexpensive cotton
fabric. Draw the shape in pencil first,
and then go over it in gold paint.

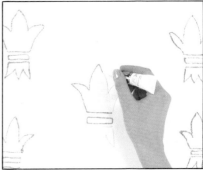

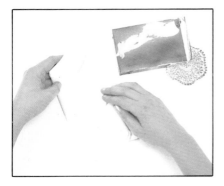

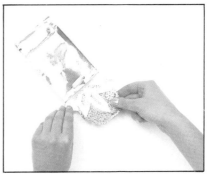

To echo the shape of the fleur-de-lys
symbol you can dress up your table
napkins as shown. A napkin with a
lacy edge will look best. Fold the
napkin into a square. Keeping the
lacy edge nearest to you, fold the
left- and right-hand corners in to
overlap one another. Fold the
remaining point in to meet them.

Slide the napkin, lacy edge towards
you, into a shining foil gift bag.
Because both napkin and china are
white, a lacy gold coaster was
inserted into the bag, underneath the
lace detail on the napkin to give it
more definition.

This simple idea can transform an ordinary tablecloth into something special. Choose a plain white or pastel-coloured tablecloth and artificial flowers with small blossoms. You will also need some green sewing thread and a needle.

If the flowers you have chosen have several blooms to a stem, trim them into individual sprigs. Set aside the remaining leaves.

Sew the flower sprigs to the cloth. You can use as many or as few sprigs as you wish; you could sew one or two by each place setting or, for a stunning effect, cover the whole cloth with them — leaving room for place settings and serving dishes. Place the leftover leaves with a single flower sprig on each guest's plate.

Give a touch of luxury to plain white china by using a larger gold plate underneath each dinner plate. You will need some old white china plates, about 1.5 to 2.5cm (½ to 1in) wider all around than your dinner plates, a few ivy leaves (at Christmas use holly and mistletoe as well), gold spray paint and a few gold or silver dragées.

Place the plate on a large sheet of scrap paper and spray it with gold paint, making sure that you follow the manufacturer's instructions on the can.

Lay the holly and ivy leaves on a sheet of scrap paper and coat them with gold paint. Leave them to dry for 10 to 15 minutes, and then arrange the painted leaves on the smaller white plate with an unsprayed sprig of mistletoe for contrast. Add a few silver dragées for the finishing touch.

This unusual placemat is easily made from cardboard and a wallpaper border. A black and white border has been chosen to co-ordinate with the table setting on pages 96-97. Cut a 30cm (12in) square from a sheet of thick cardboard, using a steel rule and craft knife to ensure precision.

Cut the border into four strips, allowing a little extra on each strip for trimming. Apply double-sided tape to the back of each strip, but do not peel off the protective backing yet. Lay two adjacent strips in place; where they meet at the corners, try to match the pattern repeat. Holding one strip on top of the other, cut diagonally across the corner.

Holding each strip in place along its inner edge, begin to peel back the protective paper from the double-sided tape, as shown. Rub a soft cloth along the border as you peel to stick it in place.

Attractive and simple to make these PVC (vinyl) placemats will also readily wipe clean. Cut a 30cm (12in) square from a sheet of thick cardboard. Take the diagonal measurement of the square — 42.5cm (17in) for this size mat — and mark a square of that size on the wrong side of the PVC; cut it out.

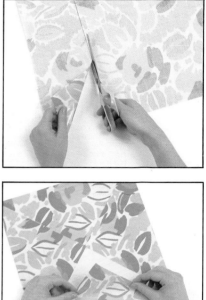

Place the cardboard square diagonally on the larger square of PVC. Spread a strong glue all over the cardboard and also on the exposed triangles of PVC. Allow them to dry until tacky.

Fold each triangle of PVC into the centre of the cardboard square so that they all meet. Press them firmly in place on the surface with a soft cloth to ensure that there are no air bubbles.

Delicate lace edging and pastel
ribbon give a pretty, feminine
look to a place setting. Use a plain
white handkerchief, or hem a piece of
fabric about 30cm (12in) square. Cut
a length of lace trimming
approximately 130cm (50in) long,
and sew it around the edge of the
fabric, gathering it at each corner
and joining the ends neatly.

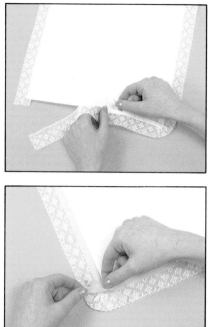

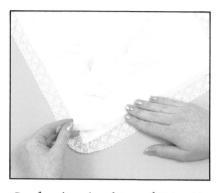

Cut four lengths of 1cm- (³/₈in)-wide
ribbon and stick them down along
the join with double-sided tape. (See
page 66 for instructions on mitring
corners.)

Cut a 20cm (8in) length of ribbon
and tie it in a bow; trim the ends
neatly. Attach it to the corner of the
mat with double-sided tape, or sew it
on with a few stitches. The ribbon
can easily be removed when the mat
needs washing.

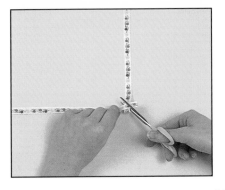

Jolly up a plastic or paper tablecloth for a children's party by using colourful strips of ribbon to mark out individual place settings. All you need, besides the tablecloth, is 1.3m (50in) of patterned ribbon for each setting and some double-sided tape.

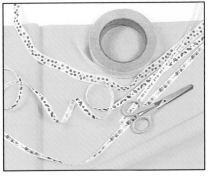

For each setting draw a 30cm (12in) square on the tablecloth. Use a ruler and set square (right-angled triangle) for accuracy. Cut the ribbon into four equal lengths. Stick tape onto the back of each ribbon and remove the backing. Stick the ribbon onto the cloth, overlapping it at the corners as shown and smoothing it just enough to hold it in place.

Where the ribbons overlap, at the corners, lift them gently and cut diagonally across them to give a neatly mitred corner. When you have trimmed each corner, run a finger along the ribbons, sticking them firmly in place.

GLITTER TREE PLACEMAT

T his sparkling placemat is an obvious winner for Christmas. First draw a Christmas tree on the reverse (matt) side of a piece of shiny green cardboard. The length should be about 10cm (4in) longer than the diameter of your dinner plate and the width about 20cm (8in) wider. Cut out the mat using a craft knife and a steel ruler.

Add 'ornaments' by sticking tiny baubles to the tips of the tree using strong glue.

Cut out or buy a star shape to put at the top of the tree. Finally, stick small silver stars over the mat. Or, if you prefer, just scatter the stars freely over the mat, first positioning each mat on the table.

—— COLOUR-FLECKED PLACEMAT ——

The perfect solution if you can't find tablemats in the right colour — paint your own, using plain cork tablemats and two colours of water-based paint. For applying the paint you will need an artist's paintbrush and a natural sponge.

Paint the cork mat all over with the lighter-coloured paint. Allow it to dry. If the colour is very pale you may need to apply a second coat.

Dip the sponge into a saucer containing the colour; dab it a few times on a piece of scrap paper to remove any excess paint. Sponge the mat all over, allowing the first paint colour to show through. When the paint is dry apply a coat of clear polyurethane varnish for protection.

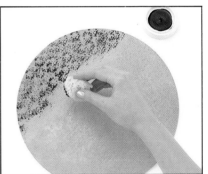

Convenient and stylish, too, this placemat roll wraps up each person's cutlery and napkin until needed. For each roll you will need a quilted cotton placemat and matching napkin and three co-ordinating ribbons, about 55cm (22in) long.

Lay the placemat flat, wrong side up. Lay the napkin and cutlery on top, then roll them up together as shown.

Trim the ends of the ribbons diagonally. Lay the roll on top of the ribbons and tie them around it into a bow.

Napkins are a necessary element of all table settings, however informal. Whether you use starched damask napkins for a formal dinner or disposable paper napkins for a buffet lunch, it is worthwhile putting a bit of thought into their presentation. In this section you will find many different ways to give your napkins an individual touch, including a number of napkin folds. These ingenious constructions often resemble origami, but are not as complicated as they look. The most important requirement for folding napkins is that they should be well starched and pressed. A spray starch will simplify the process.

The floral theme of this table setting is reminiscent of afternoon tea in an old-fashioned country garden and was inspired by the rose-patterned china. In keeping with the floral theme, the napkin is placed in a simple paper wrapper decorated with a flower motif. A cotton napkin is shown, but a paper napkin would work equally well.

Here's a quick and simple way to dress up a plain napkin for afternoon tea. All you need is a square paper doily, preferably in a colour contrasting with the napkin, and a floral motif. Begin by folding the napkin into a triangle.

Fold the doily diagonally. To create a 'spine' to allow for the thickness of the napkin, unfold the doily and make another crease about 1cm ($^3/_8$in) from the first fold.

Cut out a Victorian scrap or other floral motif and glue it to the centre of the smaller (top) side of the doily. Insert the napkin.

LOTUS BLOSSOM

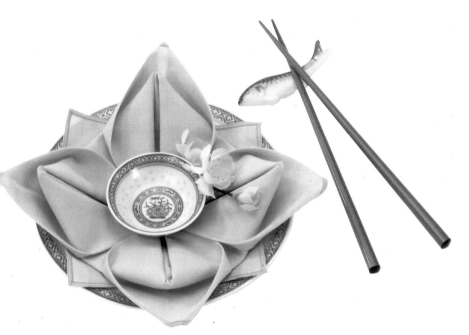

This pretty design is not as difficult to create as it may appear. The technique is similar to that used in folding the origami 'fortune cookies' so popular with children. Lay the napkin flat, and begin by folding each of the four corners into the centre.

Repeat this same procedure, drawing the corners inwards to make an even smaller square. Then turn the napkin over and repeat for a third time, holding the corners down in the centre to keep them in place.

Still keeping your finger on the centre, reach behind the napkin to one of the corners tucked underneath, and draw this gently outwards as shown until it peaks out beyond the corner of the square. Repeat the process with all four flaps to form the petals. Finally, reaching underneath again, pull out the four single flaps to make the sepals.

This elegant napkin fold is easier to produce than it looks. First fold the napkin in half diagonally, then bring the left- and right-hand corners up to meet at the apex.

Turn the napkin over, and fold the lower corner up slightly as shown.

Fold the left- and right-hand corners underneath the napkin on a slight diagonal, pressing the folds lightly in place.

A crisply starched napkin is required for this pretty fold. Lay the napkin flat. Fold two edges to meet in the centre as shown. Then fold the half nearest you across the centre line and over on the top of the other half, to form a long, thin rectangle.

Fold the right-hand end of the rectangle in towards the centre, and with another fold double it back on itself as shown. Repeat with the left-hand side so that the double folds meet in the centre.

Pull the right-hand back corner across to the left, bringing the front edge across the centre line to form a triangle. Anchoring the right hand side of the triangle with one hand, use the other hand to fold the corner back to its original position, thus creating the 'wings' of the arrangement. Repeat the process on the left-hand side.

Fold the napkin twice to form a square and position it with the loose corners at the top right. Fold the top corner back diagonally to meet the lower left corner, then turn it back on itself as shown. Continue to fold the corner back and forth to create a 'concertina' effect along the diagonal strip of napkin.

Lift the next layer of fabric from the top right-hand corner and repeat the process described above to create two parallel strips with zigzag edges.

Pick the napkin up in both hands with the zigzag folds in the centre. Fold it in half diagonally to form a triangle, keeping the pleats on the outside. Take the right-hand and left-hand corners of the triangle and curl them back, tucking one into the other to secure them. Stand the napkin upright on a plate as shown.

For best results use a crisply starched napkin to make this attractive fold. First fold the napkin lengthwise into three to form a long rectangle. Lay it horizontally with the free edge away from you, and fold the left- and right-hand ends in to meet in the centre.

Fold down the top right- and left-hand corners to meet in the centre, forming a point. Take the napkin in both hands and flip it over towards you so that the point is facing you and the flat side of the napkin is uppermost.

Lift the sides and pull them over towards one another to form a cone shape. Tuck the left-hand corner into the right-hand corner to secure it. Turn the napkin around and place it on a plate as shown in the main picture.

Fold the napkin in half to form a crease along the centre line. Then open the napkin out again. Fold one half of the napkin lengthwise into three by bringing the top edge of the square inwards to the centre line and then folding it back on itself as shown. Repeat with the second half.

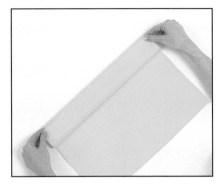

Fold the napkin in half lengthwise by tucking one half under the other along the centre line. Lay the resulting strip flat with the three folded edges facing you. Mark the centre of this strip with a finger and fold the right-hand edge in towards the centre and back on itself as shown. Repeat with the left-hand side.

Pull the top left-hand corner across towards the top right-hand corner to create a triangle, pressing down gently along the folds to hold them in place. Repeat with the remaining left-hand folds, and then do the same with all the right-hand folds. Ease the folds open slightly and display the napkin with the centre point facing the guest.

This mitre-shaped fold can be displayed either on a flat surface (as above) or in a glass, cup or soup bowl, which allows the flaps to drape gracefully over the sides. Begin by folding the napkin diagonally to form a triangle, then pull each corner up to the apex as shown to form a square.

Turn the napkin over so that the free edges lie towards you. Pull the two top flaps up and away from you; then fold the remaining two flaps back in the same way to form a triangle.

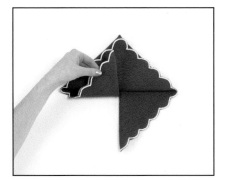

Carefully turn the napkin over once more, and pull the two outer corners together so that they overlap; tuck one flap into the folds of the other to hold them in place. Finally, turn the front of the 'hat' to face you, position the napkin upright and pull the loose flaps down as shown in the main picture.

This highly effective design benefits from a well-starched napkin and is very easy to make. Begin by folding the napkin in half lengthwise and then fold one end of the oblong backwards and forwards in concertina- or accordion-style folds, until just past the halfway point.

Holding the folds firmly together, fold the napkin lengthwise down the middle to bring both ends of the 'concertina' together. Keeping the folds in position in one hand, fold the loose flap of the napkin over across the diagonal.

Push the flap underneath the support as shown to balance the napkin, and, letting go of the pleats, allow the fan to fall into position.

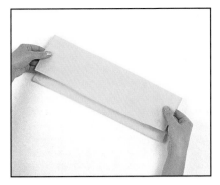

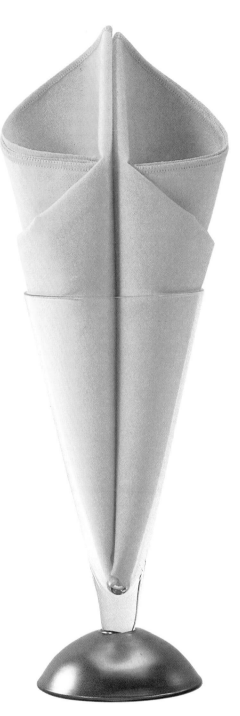

This design looks best in a conical glass but can be adapted for a wider-based container. Although it takes a little more practice than most, it is worth the effort. First lay the napkin flat and fold it in three lengthwise. Position it as shown, with the free edge on top.

Take hold of the top left-hand and right-hand corners of the napkin with the index finger and thumb of each hand. Roll the corners diagonally towards you as shown.

Without releasing your hold on the napkin, continue to roll the corners inwards in one sweeping movement by swivelling both hands and napkin down, up and over until your hands are together palms uppermost. By now the napkin should be rolled into two adjacent flutes. Release your hands and place the napkin in a glass, arranging it neatly.

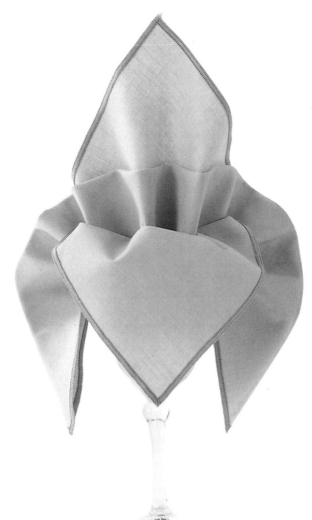

This graceful fold is easier than it looks. Lay the napkin flat and fold it in half diagonally to form a triangle. Position it with the folded edge towards you. Bring the top corner towards you, so that the point overlaps the folded edge slightly. Carefully turn the napkin over and repeat with the other corner.

Pleat the napkin evenly across from left to right, in accordion- or concertina-style, folds. Holding the straight edge of the 'concertina' firmly in position, arrange the napkin in a glass. Pull the front layer of the top point towards you, creating a pointed flap over the front of the glass.

This pretty design is ideally suited to teatime settings. Begin by folding the napkin into four — left to right, top to bottom — to form a small square. Then fold the four loose corners back across the diagonal to form a triangle.

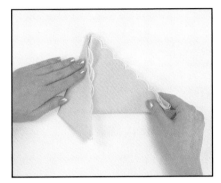

Holding the napkin firmly at the apex, fold one of the outer corners over and towards you as shown, so that it overlaps the base of the triangle. Repeat with the second corner so that the edges of both flaps meet down the centre of the napkin.

Turn the napkin over and fold the protruding flaps back over the base of the triangle. Then fold the triangle in half by pulling one of the corners over to meet the other. Finally, holding both corners firmly together, turn the napkin upright and pull the four loose corners upwards as shown in the main picture.

This simple fold looks elegant placed in a wineglass. Open the napkin flat. Fold it in half diagonally to form a triangle, and place the folded edge towards you. Place your index finger on the centre of this edge. Using the top layer of fabric only, bring the apex down to meet the left-hand corner.

Again working with the top layer only, bring the far corner down and across to the bottom left-hand corner.

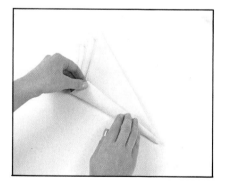

Bring the remaining top corner down and across to the lower left corner as before, forming a triangle once more. Splay the folds slightly, then turn the napkin over so that the folds are underneath. Lift the edge and roll the napkin into a loose cone shape as shown, stopping about halfway across. Fold up the bottom point and insert the napkin in the glass.

CANDLE FOLD

T his tall candle-shade fold looks especially good if the napkin has a contrasting border. Begin by laying the napkin flat. Fold it in half diagonally to form a triangle. Turn up the folded edge about 3cm (1¼in), then turn the napkin over so that the fold is underneath.

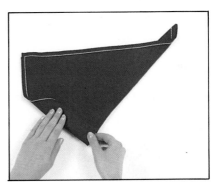

Starting at the left-hand corner, roll the napkin to form a cylindrical shape.

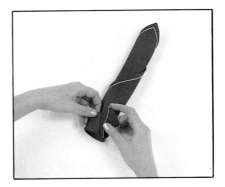

Tuck in the end to hold the roll in place. Finally, fold down the front corner at the top as shown in the main picture.

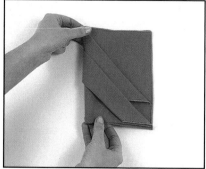

This design is perfect for a smart buffet. Fold the napkin in half, and then fold it again to form a square. Take one layer of fabric from the 'open' corner, and fold it diagonally over three times, with the final crease across the centre. Fold the second layer of fabric in the same way, making slightly shallower folds, and tuck it under the first fold.

Fold the left- and right-hand sides to the underside, leaving a central panel in which to place the cutlery. Or use the napkin as it is (without the cutlery inside) for a sit-down meal.

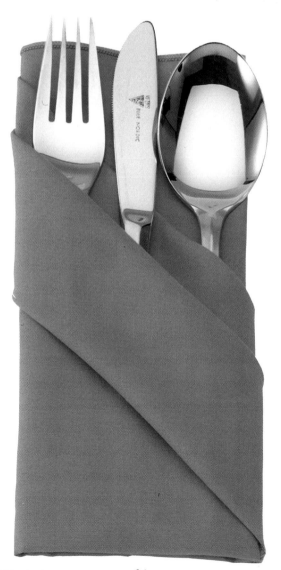

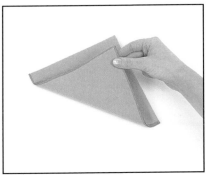

This simple napkin fold is embellished with a few artificial flowers tucked into the pocket. Fold the napkin in half and then in half again to form a square; then fold it across the diagonal to form a triangle.

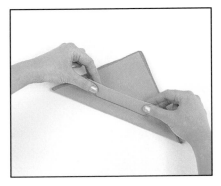

Position the napkin as shown with the four loose corners uppermost. Working with the top layer only, fold it down several times to make a cuff at the bottom.

Fold the next (single) corner over so that the tip touches the top edge of the cuff. Fold the next two corners over to form three tiers. Finally, turn the right and left corners of the triangle to the underside and overlap them. Position the napkin as shown in the main picture and insert the flowers.

This simple place setting is perfect for a Thanksgiving or Harvest Festival dinner. Use a sisal or straw placemat and a plain white napkin. For the decoration you will need a selection of dried flowers and grasses and three lengths of beige or wheat-coloured ribbon, each about 50cm (20in) long.

Tie the lengths of ribbon together at one end. Plait them until the plait is long enough to tie around the napkin twice with a little left over.

Group the bunch of dried flowers and grasses together, securing them with thread or twine. Fold the napkin in half twice to form a long, thin rectangle. Lay the flowers on top of the napkin. Wind the plaited ribbon around the napkin and flowers twice and tie the ends under the napkin.

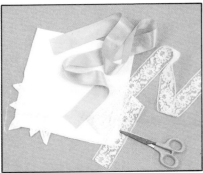

I deal for a wedding or anniversary
dinner, this lacy napkin bow is not
only pretty but also easy to make.
The napkins themselves should be
pretty, preferably with a lace detail
around the edge. For each napkin
you will need about 90cm (1yd) of
wide satin ribbon and the same
amount of insertion lace.

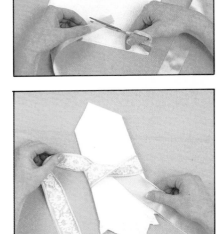

For best results, the napkin should be
starched and well ironed and folded
into quarters. To cut decorative
points for the ribbons and lace, fold
the ends as shown and cut them
diagonally.

Fold under two corners of the napkin
to overlap in the centre, forming the
shape shown here. Iron the folds flat.
Lay the ribbon and lace flat, wrong
side up, with the ribbon on top.
Place the napkin on top and tie the
ribbon and lace around it in a bow.

This original napkin fold makes a pretty circular shape and is embellished with a bead and ribbon trimming. Paint a plain 25mm (1in) wooden bead with a water-based paint to match your napkin. Then paint on a pattern with a harmonizing or contrasting colour. Allow the paint to dry between coats.

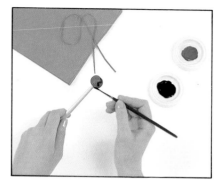

Fold the napkin in half once along its length, and then pleat it accordion-fashion along its length, making sure the folds are the same size.

Thread a length of thin ribbon through the bead and tie it to hold the bead in place. Wrap the ribbon around the centre of the napkin, and tie it in a neat bow just below the bead. Fan the napkin out so that it forms a full circle.

TASSEL NAPKIN RING

This tasselled napkin ring is ideal for a special occasion. You will need two tassels and approximately 40cm (16in) of cord per napkin, and a strong fabric glue. Attach the tassels to the cord by wrapping the loop around the cord and pulling the tassels through it.

Make the ring by feeding the cord through both loops of the tassels twice more. Make sure that the ring is large enough to slip easily over the napkin.

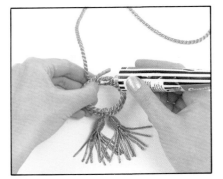

Using a strong glue, secure the ends of the cord to the back of the ring. Lay one end along the back and trim it. Having applied the glue to the inside of the ring as shown, wrap the remaining end over the cords, covering the trimmed end. Cut the remaining piece of cord on the inside, and clamp it in position until it is dry.

This charming flower-trimmed napkin ring adds a touch of elegance to a table setting and is very easy to make. Bend a short length of florists' wire into a circle; twist the ends together to secure them.

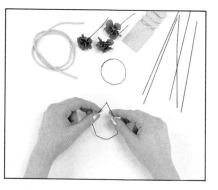

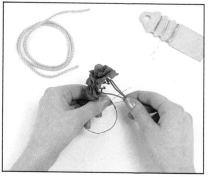

Wind some fine fuse wire around one or two small silk flowers — chosen to co-ordinate with your china and table linen. Then twist the ends of the fuse wire around the circle of florist's wire to hold the flowers in place.

For covering the ring choose a fine ribbon or decorative braid. Hold one end in place with one hand, and use the other hand to twist the braid around the circle to cover it completely, beginning and ending underneath the flowers. Secure the ends with glue. Insert the napkin and add a fresh flower for the finishing touch.

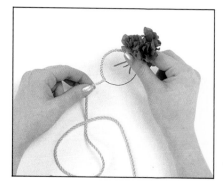

For a touch of frivolity, tie your table napkins in several shades of net. For each napkin cut three different-coloured rectangles of net, 45 by 35cm (18in by 13in). Fold each piece crosswise into three equal sections.

Fold the napkin twice to form a square, and then fold it diagonally to form a triangle. Now roll it lengthwise.

Place the lengths of net on top of each other; tie them around the napkin and fan out the ends.

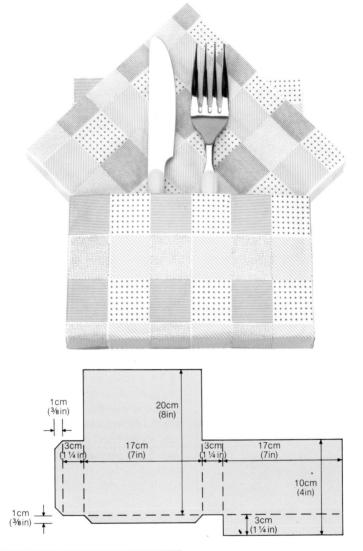

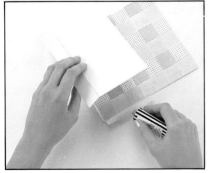

To make this attractive napkin box, draw the above diagram to the measurements indicated. Cut it out with a sharp knife and score the folds marked with a dotted line. Cut out a piece of water-resistant paper or PVC, approximately 21 by 19cm (8½ by 7½in). Stick it down onto the front inside area of the box, and fold overlapping paper to the back of the card; glue it in place.

Apply glue to the sides and base of the box and stick the box together. Cut out a second piece of paper 26 by 12.5cm (10½ by 5in) and glue it onto the outside front and sides of the box, snipping the corners to enable you to tuck the free edges in. Finally, cut a third piece of paper 20 by 17cm (8 by 7in) to glue to the back of the box and cover all the untidy edges.

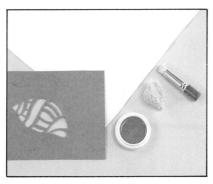

If you can't find a ready-made napkin to complement your china or decorative scheme, you can easily decorate your own with a stencil design. All you need is a plain napkin or a hemmed square of fabric, a stencil motif — either bought (quilters' suppliers have them) or original, a natural sponge and some fabric paint.

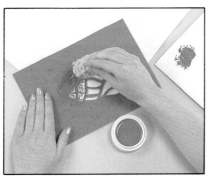

Position the stencil on the napkin. Mix the paint in a saucer or palette. Dip the sponge into the paint and dab it on a piece of scrap paper to remove the excess. As an alternative to a sponge you can use a stencil brush, which will give a slightly different effect. It is worthwhile trying both to see which best suits your design.

You can either hold the stencil in place with your fingers or fasten it with tape. Dab paint through the stencil onto the fabric, taking care that it doesn't seep under the edges. When the paint is dry, fix it following the manufacturer's instructions.

Place cards have traditionally been used to organize the seating at large banquets. Because these days most people have neither the time to cater for, nor the space to accommodate, a large number of guests, place cards are not often needed. It is a pity, however, that we don't use place cards more often. Instead of thinking of them as rather formal and ceremonious, we should see them as adding an element of fun and individuality to a table. When you have gone to the trouble of devising a theme for your table, it's a nice idea to extend the theme to include place cards.

A harlequin theme prevails in this
striking table setting — perfect for a
fancy-dress party. The chequered square
place card sits in a black-stemmed cocktail
glass, with a pink streamer tumbling
gracefully over the edge. You can also
make papier-mâché harlequin masks for
each guest; or you can just make two and
place them back to back to form a
centrepiece.

HARLEQUIN PLACE CARD

$\mathbf{M}$ake cocktail glasses look extra smart with this chequered place card. It matches the black and white setting on pages 96-97. First cut a 7.5cm (3in) square from a piece of stiff white cardboard. Use a pencil and ruler to mark off 2.5cm (1in) divisions and join these up to form a grid. Colour in alternate squares with a black felt pen to give a chequer-board pattern.

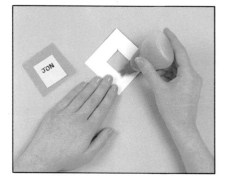

On a 5cm (2in) square of cardboard write the name. Cut out a 6cm-(2½in)-square piece of pink net fabric; set it aside. Using a sharp craft knife, cut out the centre of the chequered card to leave a hole 2.5cm (1in) square. Turn the card over and apply some glue around the edges of the hole.

Place the piece of net over the card with the name, and hold them together in one hand while positioning the chequered card diagonally over the top. Press firmly to apply the glue to all three surfaces. Leave the card to dry for a few minutes.

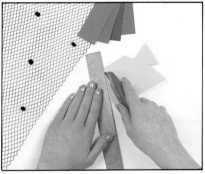

This original place card is simple to make using different colours of stiff paper and scraps of net. First cut a rectangle out of lightweight cardboard, twice the depth of the finished card; fold it in half. Using a craft knife and a steel ruler, cut sections of the card away to create an irregular edge. The cards can be any shape; in fact, it is more fun if they all look a little different.

From the coloured paper cut the letters to spell each guest's name. Don't try to cut rounded shapes, as this is more difficult. It may be easier to make some letters from two pieces. For a letter A, for example, cut a V shape, turn it upside down, and add a separate strip for the crossbar. Glue the letters in place.

Cut irregular pieces from a scrap of net, and lightly glue these in place over the name. Place each card on a plate on top of a folded napkin, as shown.

This unusual place marker is perfect for an Easter table. Pierce the top of an egg with a pin and the bottom with a darning needle, plunging the needle well in to break the yolk. Hold the egg over a cup and blow through the smaller hole, forcing the contents out through the bottom. Rinse the shell under a tap. Pencil on the name and design.

Using a white water-based paint, fill in all the areas that will be painted in light colours. This will help to ensure that the colours are true.

Use your chosen colours to paint over the white areas. There's no need to worry if the outline is untidy, since the darker background will cover all the edges. Finally, paint the background in a dark colour.

CUTOUT PLACE CARD

Bold cutout letters complement a modern table setting. Use white cardboard against coloured napkins, or vice versa. On a sheet of tracing paper, draw two guidelines about 8cm (3in) apart. This will be the height of the letters. Use a ruler to help you draw the name, making sure that each letter is linked to the next.

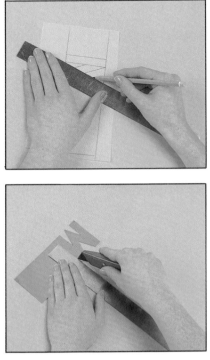

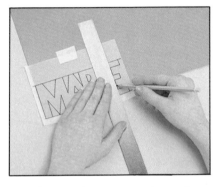

Lay the traced name on a sheet of thin cardboard, and secure it in place with masking tape. Draw over all the letters again, using a hard lead pencil or ball-point pen to make an imprint on the cardboard.

Remove the tracing paper. Cut the name out of the cardboard, using a ruler and a sharp craft knife. Take care to follow the imprinted lines exactly, for an incorrect cut might result in the letters becoming detached from each other.

COLLAGE PLACE CARD

This collage place card can be made from wrapping paper and scraps of plain stiff paper. Select a gift-wrapping paper with a design that is appropriate to the theme of your party and plain paper in a harmonizing colour. Cut a rectangle of the plain paper about 14 by 9cm (5½ by 3½in) and fold it in half as shown.

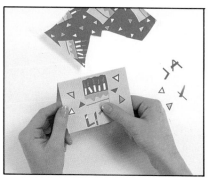

Cut around the shape you have decided to use and stick this to the card with double-sided tape or glue.

Stick additional shapes onto the card as desired. Put double-sided tape onto the back of a small area of the wrapping paper, and cut thin strips with which to make up the names. Peel off the backing and attach the strips to the card to form the letters.

RICEPAPER FANS PLACE CARD

Tiny pleated fans decorate these pastel place cards. From pale pastel stiff paper cut a rectangle about 9 by 12cm (3½ by 5in). From darker paper cut a rectangle about 5mm (¼in) shorter and narrower. Cut several thin strips from a sheet of ricepaper, and fold them concertina-style as shown.

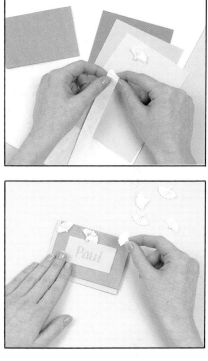

Allowing 10 or 12 folds per fan, snip the folded strips into several pieces. Pinch them at one end to form tiny fans. Fold the two rectangles in half, and place the darker one over the other. Lightly glue them in place. Cut a small rectangle from the paler paper for the name; glue it onto the front of the card.

Put several dabs of glue on the card and glue the fans in place as shown.

KITE PLACE CARDS

These colourful place cards are perfect for a children's party. For each kite you will need stiff paper in two colours. From each colour cut two rectangles, each 10 by 15cm (4 by 6in). Draw a line down the centre, then another line at right angles across it, 5cm (2in) from one end. Join up the points, then cut off the four corners; set them aside.

Use two of the corners of the red card to decorate the yellow kite, glueing them in place as shown. Similarly, use two of the leftover pieces of the yellow card to decorate the red kite. Write the name on each kite.

Cut out squares of coloured tissue, allowing three for each kite. On the back of each kite, glue a 40cm (16in) strip of thin ribbon. Pinch the squares of tissue together in the centre and tie the ribbon around them. Cut a small strip of cardboard, fold it in two and glue it to the back of the kite; use this hook to attach the kite to a glass.

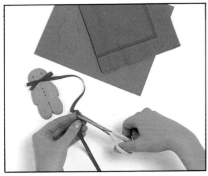

Sure to be a hit with children, each little gingerbread man is tucked into a napkin and has his own place card 'shadow'. Copy the shape of the gingerbread man onto stiff coloured paper; set it aside. Using a length of thin satin ribbon, tie a bow around the neck of the gingerbread man, leaving an end about 15cm (6in) long.

Cut the ends of the ribbon into points by folding them double and cutting a diagonal across the fold. Cut the drawn shape from the coloured paper.

Write the child's name on the shape. Apply a dab of glue and stick the card shape onto the ribbon. Fold back one corner of a bright-coloured paper napkin to make an envelope for the gingerbread man.

VALENTINE PLACE CARD

Heart-shaped place cards are perfect for a romantic dinner or Valentine's Day supper. Using the template provided, trace heart shapes onto shiny red and plain white lightweight cardboard, and carefully cut them out.

Write the person's name on the white heart. Punch or cut a hole at the top of each heart, and thread a thin red ribbon through the hole. To add the finishing touches, tie the cutlery together with a wider ribbon, making a pretty bow. Then loosely tie the place cards to the bow, securing the cutlery as shown above.

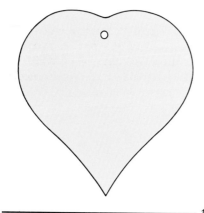

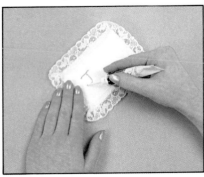

Lace is a natural choice for decorating a table for a special occasion such as a wedding anniversary. Take a rectangular piece of stiff paper and score it across the centre for the fold. Cut a piece of lace long enough to go around half the card, plus a little extra. Sew it around the edges with matching thread, gathering it at the corners.

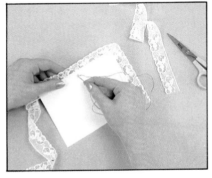

Fold the card in half so that the front half covers the tacking, and glue the two layers together as shown.

Use silver glitter paint to write the name on the front of the card. Set the card on the plate along with some pretty flowers for a buttonhole.

FLORAL PLACE CARD

This charming place card looks
especially good on floral china.
Cut the posies from Victorian floral
transfers, or from magazines, seed
catalogues or greeting cards.

Cut a piece of thin white cardboard
about 10 by 8cm (4 by 3in). Group
the flower shapes on the card as
shown. Once you have created a
pleasing arrangement, glue the
shapes in place on the card. Set it
aside to dry.

Cut a strip of pastel-coloured stiff
paper, and write the name on it. Set
it aside. Cut around the flower
shapes, leaving a 1cm (½in) strip of
white cardboard along the bottom.
Fold this backwards to form a stand
for the place card. A tiny posy of
dried lavender can be placed on each
plate alongside the card.

For a traditional Hogmanay or Burns Night celebration, make tartan place cards for your guests. Use plaid ribbon and either white or coloured lightweight cardboard, and add a kilt pin for the finishing touch.

Cut a rectangle of cardboard about 10 by 12cm (4 by 5in), or a size to fit the plate. Fold it in half, and write the name on the left-hand side. Cut a piece of ribbon to edge the card front and back, allowing a little extra to turn under the edges.

Stick ribbon onto the card with fabric glue, folding the excess underneath as shown. Pin the kilt pin through the ribbon and card to complete the authentically Scottish look.

This pastry place marker has a Christmas theme, but you could easily use a different shape for another occasion. Make the dough by mixing three parts of white flour to one of salt, a spoonful of glycerine and enough cold water to give a good consistency. Knead the pastry for about 10 minutes, then roll it flat on a floured surface.

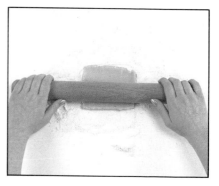

Cut out the shapes with a sharp knife or a pastry cutter. Remember to make a hole for the ribbon. Bake the pastry in the normal way.

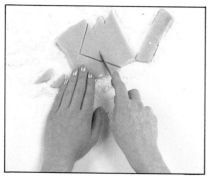

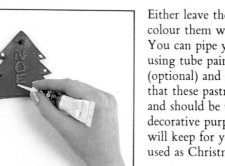

Either leave the shapes plain or colour them with water-based paint. You can pipe your guests' names on using tube paint. Varnish the shapes (optional) and attach a ribbon. Note that these pastry shapes are not edible and should be used only for decorative purposes; however, they will keep for years. They can also be used as Christmas tree ornaments.

Essential wear at any children's party, these hats can also serve as place cards. First cut the hats out of lightweight cardboard — a small circle and a rectangular piece for the fez and a semi-circular piece, about 15cm (6in) in diameter, for the conical hat. Glue the sides together to form a tube and a cone, and attach the top circle to the fez with tape. Cover the hats in crepe paper.

Make pompoms (see page 119) for both hats and attach them with glue or double-sided tape. Make a frill for the conical hat by cutting two lengths of crepe paper about 5cm (2in) deep and long enough to go around the edge of the rim. Neatly cut narrow strips about 2cm (¾in) deep on either side of the length to create a fringe. Staple the two layers of 'fringe' onto the rim of the hat.

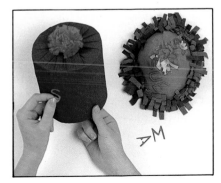

Cut out paper letters from contrasting-coloured paper and glue names onto the front of each hat.

Placing a gift by each table setting is an age-old tradition which is particularly popular at Christmas or for a children's party. Your gifts needn't be anything expensive or elaborate, but they will delight your guests and serve as mementoes of the occasion. This section includes a variety of ideas, from home-made crackers to pretty muslin bags containing sweet-smelling lavender. Chocolates and other sweets are popular, and you can package them in different ways depending on the occasion. Heart-shaped boxes are a must for Valentine's Day, and shiny gold or silver boxes add elegance to a formal dinner table.

Traditional red and green are used for
this Christmas table setting, and
Christmas tree shapes are the prevailing
theme, appearing in everything from the
placemats to the cake. Gifts include
home-made Christmas crackers, wrapped
in red and green crepe paper, and
miniature Christmas stockings, each
containing a jolly chocolate teddy bear.

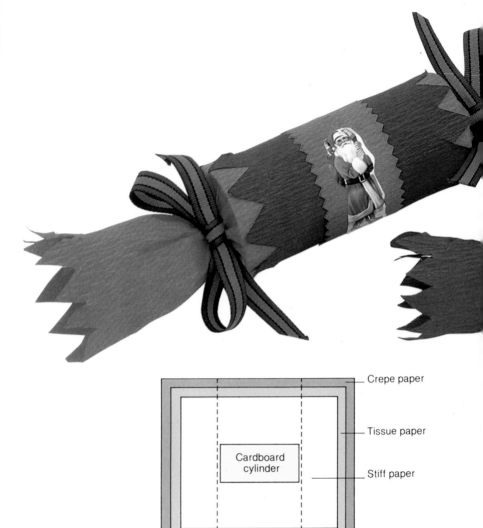

Crepe paper

Tissue paper

Cardboard cylinder

Stiff paper

Crackers are usually associated with Christmas, but they can be used at any time of the year. The diagram above shows the materials required for a cracker: crepe paper for the outside, tissue paper for the lining, and stiff paper and a cardboard cylinder to hold the cracker in shape.

Cut the paper layers as indicated above. Roll them around the tube, and stick them in place securely with either glue or tape. A friction strip can be placed between the stiff paper and cylinder to provide a 'bang' when the cracker is pulled.

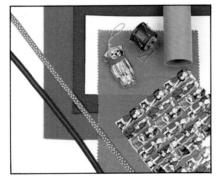

Gather the paper together at one end and tie it with ribbon. Leave the other end open to drop in the gift, hat and joke of your choice. Tie this end and trim the ribbons neatly.

Cut a zigzag edge in the paper at both ends; or leave the ends plain, if you prefer.

Add the final decorative touches — in this case, contrasting layers of crepe paper and a paper motif.

RED HOT CRACKERS

Stylish black and white paper decorates these modern bright red crackers. Follow the instructions on pages 114-115 for assembling the basic cracker, using red crepe paper for the outer layer. Cut a decorative edging, if desired, at both ends.

Cut a rectangular piece of black and white gift wrap or other patterned paper, long enough to go around the cylinder with a small overlap. Cut the long edges to match the ends of the cracker. Wrap the strip around the cracker and glue along the join.

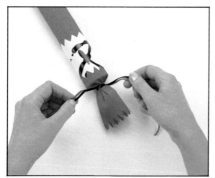

Tie one end with two lengths of fine ribbon in black, white and/or red. Insert the gift into the cylinder and tie the other end. Add place cards or write names on the crackers if appropriate.

This old-fashioned cracker makes a charming addition to the table. Follow the basic step-by-step guide for making a cracker on pages 114-115, cutting the outer crepe paper layer 5cm (2in) short of the recommended size. Make up the difference by attaching strips of paper doilies as shown, using double-sided tape or glue to secure the strips at each end.

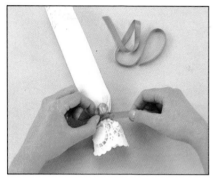

Cover the join of doily and crepe paper at one end with a length of ribbon in a contrasting colour, tied in a bow. Insert the chosen motto and small gifts in the cylinder. Tie the other end as before, and trim the ribbon ends neatly.

Cut out a traditional Victorian scrap or motif from an old Christmas card or other greeting card, and glue it to the cracker. Alternatively, you may be able to purchase attractive Victorian-style motifs from a stationer's.

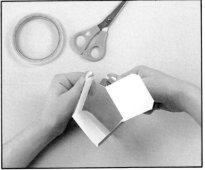

This elegant little box is
ideal for wrapping a special gift.
First draw the diagram to the
specified measurements, then trace it.
Tape the tracing to the wrong side
of medium-weight cardboard with
masking tape and draw over the
outline with a ballpoint pen to make
a light indentation in the cardboard.
Cut around the outline.

Score the fold lines carefully with
scissor points and fold the box
accordingly. Apply glue to the flaps
and join the box together as shown.
Allow it to dry thoroughly before
using it.

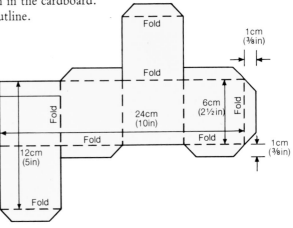

Fold

Fold

1cm
(⅜in)

6cm
(2½in)

Fold

Fold

24cm
(10in)

Fold

Fold

1cm
(⅜in)

12cm
(5in)

Fold

If you have a plain gift box and want to jazz it up a bit, this tissue paper pompom is just the thing. Fold the tissue to get at least 12 layers, measuring 7cm (3in) square. Using a cup or glass, mark a circle on the paper, and cut it out. Staple the layers together at the centre.

Cut strips into the centre, making them about 5mm (¼in) wide at the edge and stopping short of the staple. Fluff up the tissue paper to form a pompom, and glue it to the box. If you wish to make your own box, copy the template below, referring to the page opposite for further instructions.

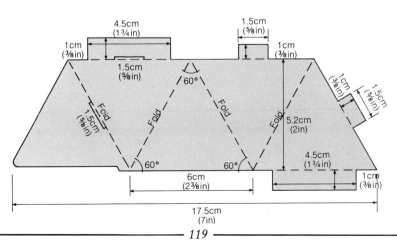

VALENTINE GIFT BOXES

Decorating your own gift boxes for sweets or a tiny present adds a festive touch to a special occasion. These red and black boxes contain chocolate hearts for a Valentine's Day dinner. For the smaller box, first paint a plain heart-shaped wooden box red. Use a fine-bristle artist's brush to add black dots all over the outside of the box.

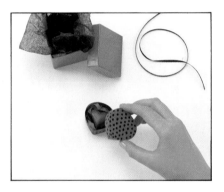

Place one or more chocolates in the box, along with some red ribbon for padding. Tie the lid in place with thin black ribbon.

Add an individual touch to a plain red cardboard box by lining it with black tissue and tying black and white spotted ribbon around it.

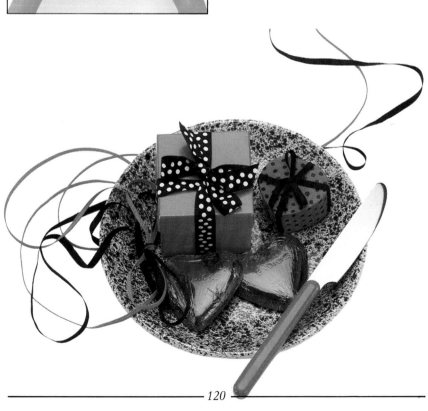

A stunning, yet simple, idea for a festive dinner party, these net bags contain sweets for your guests. Cut a large gold doily in half. Fold the edges around to meet one another, creating a cone shape, and then secure them with tape.

Cut out a square of black dressmaker's or milliner's net. Use it double for a fuller effect. Holding the net square in one hand, place the gold doily cone into it. Place three or four black and gold dragées in the cone.

Gather the net and doily cone into a 'waist', leaving some extra at the top. Secure it with sewing thread, wrapped tightly around it several times, or with an elastic band. Cut equal lengths of thin gold and black ribbon, and tie them around the waist and into a bow at the front.

This pretty favour will scent a summer table and can be taken home by a guest after the meal. Group together five or six flowers to form a small posy. Holding them firmly in one hand, tie the stems together with a length of fuse wire.

Fold the smaller of two doilies in half and set it aside. With a pair of scissors snip a small hole in the centre of the larger doily and push the stems of the posy through it.

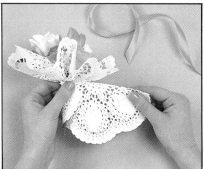

Gather the large doily together around the flower-heads and hold it firmly in place. With the other hand, wrap the folded doily around the stems, making sure it overlaps the excess gathers of the large doily. Use a pin or tape to hold it in place. Tie a piece of satin ribbon around the posy to conceal the joins.

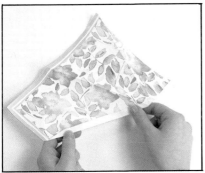

Pretty floral giftwrap is used to make this conical envelope for holding sweets or other party favours. Use the diagram given below as a guide for cutting out the shape. Leaving a corner to form the triangular flap, fold the paper as shown, allowing an overlap for glueing. Stick down the back flap neatly.

Attach a short length of decorative cord to the inside of the envelope, using a strong glue. Place sweets or a gift inside the bag, and stick down the flap with glue. Cover the join with a Victorian scrap or other floral motif cut from a greeting card or purchased from a stationer's.

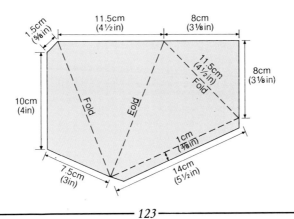

Sweet-smelling lavender sachets can be taken home by your guests and used to scent bureau drawers. You will need some dried lavender, a square of muslin, two squares of net (one white and one lilac) and a length of ribbon. To dry your own lavender, pick the stems just before the flowers open, and hang them up in a warm, dry place.

Lay the square of white net on top of the lilac square. On top of this place the square of muslin and then some lavender flowers stripped off the stem. Gather all the layers together in two hands and bunch them together in the centre.

Tie the ribbon around the fabric and into a bow. Trim off any excess ribbon, and place the bag on a plate. Add a couple of fresh flowers or sprigs of lavender as further decoration.

Pretty fabric makes the perfect wrapping for fine scented soap; watch for suitable remnants in fabric departments. Cut a 15cm (6in) square of fabric, using pinking shears for a decorative edge and to prevent fraying.

For a gift bag, place the soap in the centre of the square of fabric. Gather the corners together in the centre. Tie a contrasting ribbon around the fabric and into a bow. For an envelope, fold the four corners of the square over the soap to overlap in the centre.

Hold the flaps of the envelope in place and tie them up with a contrasting ribbon. Finish off with a large bow.

Here's a pretty — and witty — way to serve shell-or fish-shaped chocolates. (You can either buy these from some confectioners, or make them yourself using special moulds.) Cut a large doily in half. Put one half aside, and cut the other one in half again to make a quarter section; discard the remaining quarter.

Take two scallop shells, one slightly larger than the other. Place the half doily on top of the larger shell, straight edge away from you. Put the quarter doily into the smaller shell, fancy edge away from you. Trim the ends of a 25 to 30cm (10 to 12in) length of blue satin ribbon; fold the ribbon in two and place it in the large scallop shell.

Holding the ribbon in position, place the small shell in the larger one; straighten the edges of the doilies if necessary. Fill the small shell with a mixture of real shells and chocolate shells and fish shapes.

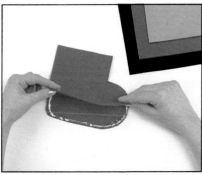

For a children's party at Christmas or any time of the year, this ingenious place marker is sure to be a winner. First, cut two boot shapes from bright-coloured felt, making sure that they are large enough to enclose a chocolate teddy or other favour. Stick the shapes together with fabric glue, leaving the top open.

From contrasting felt, cut a zigzag strip for the upper edge and some letters to make the name.

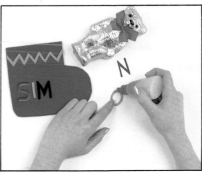

Glue the strip and the letters to the boot as shown. Finally, insert the chocolate teddy into the boot.

INDEX

ACKNOWLEDGEMENTS

The authors and publishers would like to thank the following for their help
in compiling this book:

Heal's, 196 Tottenham Court Road, London W1
Lakeland Plastics, Alexander Buildings, Windermere, Cumbria
Paperchase, 213 Tottenham Court Road, London W1
Pebeo water-based, textured and fabric paints from:
Artemis Products Ltd, 684 Mitcham Road, Croydon
Viners Cutlery, Cranborne House, Cranborne Road, Potters Bar, Hertfordshire

Photographs
Anthony Blake, page 19
The Viners Group, page 13
All other photographs in this book were taken by Steve Tanner
and are the copyright of Salamander Books Ltd.